Tanoshii

Tanoshii

Joy of Making Japanese-style
Cakes and Desserts

Yamashita Masataka

To my parents, who did not approve
of my decision to become a pastry chef
in the beginning, but who grew to see my passion
in it and have been supporting me
in every possible way ever since.

To my wife and best friend, Ami Yamashita,
for always being by my side with a smile.
She is the only person who truly understands me
and knows exactly what to say when
the going gets tough.

The Publisher would like to thank:

The Baking Loft for the use of their cooking studio and appliances
for the duration of the photography session (www.thebakingloft.com);

Francfranc for the loan of the props used in the photographs in this book.

Editor   : Lydia Leong
Designer   : Lynn Chin Nyuk Ling
Photographers : Joshua Tan (Elements by the Box) and Valiant Chow

Copyright © 2013 Marshall Cavendish International (Asia) Private Limited
An imprint of Marshall Cavendish International
Reprinted 2013, 2014

Other Marshall Cavendish Offices:

Marshall Cavendish Corporation, 99 White Plains Road, Tarrytown NY 10591-9001, USA • Marshall
Cavendish International (Thailand) Co Ltd. 253 Asoke, 12th Flr, Sukhumvit 21 Road, Klongtoey Nua,
Wattana, Bangkok 10110, Thailand • Marshall Cavendish (Malaysia) Sdn Bhd, Times Subang, Lot 46,
Subang Hi-Tech Industrial Park, Batu Tiga, 40000 Shah Alam, Selangor Darul Ehsan, Malaysia

Marshall Cavendish is a trademark of Times Publishing Limited

National Library Board, Singapore Cataloguing-in-Publication Data

Yamashita, Masataka.
Tanoshii : joy of making Japanese style cakes and desserts / Yamashita Masataka. – Singapore :
Marshall Cavendish Editions, c2013.
p. cm.
ISBN : 978-981-4398-04-6

1. Cake. 2. Desserts. 3. Cooking, Japanese. I. Title. II. Title: Joy of making Japanese style cakes
and desserts

TX773
641.860952 -- dc23   OCN807433149

Printed in Singapore by Craft Print International Ltd

Acknowledgements

I would like to thank the following people
for making this book possible:

My mentor, Keisuke Oishi, for teaching me everything I know about
pastry. He is the reason why I am the pastry chef I am today. Without
him, I would not have been able to continue in this line for more than
27 years. He has my appreciation and deepest respect.

My friend, Sharon Low, for her direct contribution to this book
as translator, and for her infectious enthusiasm, inspiration and
selflessness right from the onset of this project. Without her effort,
this book would not have been possible.

My editor, Lydia Leong, for giving me the opportunity to publish
a book in Singapore, and for her endless patience and support
throughout the process of producing this book.

The photographers, Joshua Tan and Valiant Chow, and the designer,
Lynn Chin, for making the photography session so fun. This beautiful
book is a result of their wonderful teamwork.

Introduction

First of all, I would like to thank you for your support in buying my cookbook. Let me start by sharing with you briefly about how I became a pastry chef. I was born in Nara, Japan, and from a young age, I have always loved baking. I enjoyed making beautiful cakes, sweets and pastries for my family and friends, and I found great satisfaction in knowing that a simple but well-made cake could bring so much joy and laughter to my loved ones.

Many of my peers chose to become lawyers and doctors, but I knew my heart was and will always belong in the kitchen, so I chose the unconventional route. It was not easy in the beginning, but through hard work and determination, I rose to become the executive pastry chef of the world famous Schlossgasse Mozart in Okayama, Japan. That was when I decided it was time for a new challenge and I opened Flor Patisserie in Nara, Japan.

Over the years, many of my loyal customers have asked why I did not have a cookbook to my name. The truth is I have always felt it was not the right time for me to write a cookbook as I have so much more to learn—a chef never stops learning! So it was a very humbling experience to have so many supporters request that I write a cookbook.

When I started working on this cookbook, my main challenge was picking which of my best-loved recipes to showcase, as it was my desire to share all my knowledge through this book. After all these months of hard work, with the support of my very understanding team, I have to say I am completely satisfied with this book that you now hold in your hands.

The reason why I decided to write this cookbook was simple. Through the years, many loyal customers have also asked me why baking cakes is so difficult and why their cakes always fail. I strongly believe that this need not be so! Baking should not be hard or stressful, but fun and enjoyable!

So, in a way, this cookbook is the expression of my appreciation to all my loyal customers for their continuous support through the years, and my answer to all these questions on baking. It is also a profession of my personal belief that making cakes, sweets and pastries is for everyone, from the novice home baker to the most experienced baker. I trust there is something in this cookbook for everyone.

I have included step-by-step photographs with easy-to-follow instructions for each recipe as, to me, baking is very visual, so by showing each step, it's like having me in your kitchen, beside you, guiding you every step of the way. You won't need fanciful equipment or expensive ovens to bake a good cake, just the right attitude and passion to bake.

Lastly, I will like to emphasise that baking is all about having fun in the kitchen, so don't feel demoralised when your cake fails to turn out. Instead, try again and don't give up! Remember, even the most experienced chefs may fail, but it is through failure that we come up with something even more amazing!

So do have fun trying out the various recipes in this cookbook, and remember to always enjoy the baking process. May all your cakes, sweets and pastries bring smiles and laughter to you and your loved ones!

Yamashita Masataka

Baking Equipment

Baking Tins

Choose baking tins made of stainless steel as they last longer. Both round and square baking tins are used in this book. For round cakes, 15-cm, 18-cm and 21-cm diameter tins are used. For square cakes, 18-cm, 24-cm and 30-cm tins are used.

Baking Trays

A 30 x 30 x 3-cm baking tray is used for the roll cake recipes in this book. If your oven is smaller, simply buy what suits your oven. The amount of batter produced in the recipe can be divided into separate moulds and baking time adjusted accordingly.

Bamboo Skewer

A thin skewer is essential for testing if a cake is adequately baked. If an inserted skewer comes out clean, you are good to go. All ovens are different, so it is incredibly important to monitor, observe and test as you go along.

Blowtorch

A blowtorch can be used to caramelise Italian meringues and sugar on the surface of crème brûlée. It is not essential, but it will allow you to give your desserts an impressive, professional-looking finish.

Citrus Juicer

This is useful for extracting juice from citrus fruit. There are many types of juicers, both manual and electric, and any type that does the job will do.

Cookie Cutters

Also known as biscuit cutters, these are used for cutting shapes from cookie/biscuit dough. Cutters are available in countless decorative shapes and are useful for churning out large batches of cookies/biscuits where simplicity and uniformity are required.

Decorating Turntable

A cake decorating turntable will allow you to decorate cakes in a more professional manner, but this is a worthwhile investment only if you intend to decorate cakes frequently.

Digital Kitchen Timer

A digital timer will help ensure baking accuracy. This is necessary only if your oven is not equipped with a timer.

Digital Scale

Precision is of utmost importance in baking, thus it is important to invest in a digital scale. Many recipes in this book call for weight measurements so I recommend using a scale that can weigh up to 5 kg and has a minimum scale unit of 1 g. Treat your scale well and never store anything on top of it. Ensure that it stays calibrated.

Grater

This is useful for grating hard cheeses, chocolate, ginger and the zest of citrus fruit. Choose a fine grater with razor sharp teeth.

Measuring Cup

A clear glass measuring cup is recommended for measuring liquid as glass can withstand heat and will not retain grease like plastic.
A 500-ml measuring cup is ideal.

Measuring Spoons

Measuring spoons are used for measuring small quantities of liquid and powder ingredients precisely. A baker's set should include ¼ tsp, ½ tsp, 1 tsp and 1 Tbsp measures. Both stainless steel and plastic measuring spoons will work well. When measuring out ingredients, be sure to level the contents for accuracy.

Mixer

Both electric stand mixers and electric handheld mixers will work for all recipes in this book, but a stand mixer will lead to more professional results. If you intend to bake seriously and frequently, invest in a good stand mixer with a stainless steel bowl that can handle even the smallest quantity of ingredients.

Mixing Bowls

Stainless steel bowls are used in professional kitchens as their conductivity means that they can be used effectively in hot or iced water baths. Avoid plastic bowls as they retain smells and grease. Mixing bowls made of glass is acceptable.

Offset Spatula

Offset spatulas have an angled edge that is useful for removing cookies from baking trays and decorating celebration cakes. Choose a thin metal spatula approximately 23 cm in length.

Parchment Paper

Parchment paper is used to line baking trays and cake pans. It is non-stick, reusable and disposable, which makes for easy cleaning. Sifting flour on parchment paper also allows for easy transfer into a mixing bowl. Parchment paper can be folded and used as a piping bag. Baked goods can also be packaged using parchment paper.

Pastry Brush

A 5-cm wide brush can be used for almost everything, from buttering small cake moulds and ramekins, to applying egg wash. Pastry brushes with natural bristles instead of silicon is preferred. Wash immediately after use and hang to dry to keep your pastry brushes in tip top condition. Replace as soon as the bristles start to shed.

Pie Cutter

This is a ring with blades that will help cut wedges from pies, tarts and quiches neatly and evenly for professional-looking results. If unavailable, a sharp serrated knife will do.

Piping Bags

Piping bags are used to decorate cakes and tarts, and for piping small amounts of batter. Select bags made of a sturdy material or use disposable ones for ease of cleaning up.

Rolling Pin

A heavy wooden pin without handles offers the most control. A 45-cm long, 3.5-cm diameter pin is ideal for working with pastry.

Rubber Spatula

A heat resistant rubber spatula would aid in mixing cake batter and folding dry ingredients into the wet. Choose one that is flexible but not flimsy.

Saucepans

In baking, saucepans are used for cooking custard creams and sauces as well as melting butter. A saucepan that is at least 11 cm deep is ideal for stirring.

Scraper

A plastic scraper is preferred for smoothing out the surface of sponge batters because of its lightness and sensitivity, while a stainless steel scraper is preferred for dividing dough.

Serrated Cake Slicer

A long serrated knife is useful for slicing sponge cakes and bread into layers without compressing it. A 30–35-cm long serrated cake slicer would suffice for most tasks.

Sieve

A large 16-cm diameter sieve with a handle is useful for straining wet ingredients as it can be suspended over a bowl. A similar sieve without a handle is useful for sifting dry ingredients onto parchment paper. A small sieve with a handle is useful for dusting icing sugar or cocoa powder over baked goods. Look for sieves with a sturdy mesh.

Tart Tins & Pie Plates

Tart tins have straight sides which may be fluted or not. A tart tin with a removable base makes unmoulding much easier and produces professional-looking results. A pie plate is a slope-sided dish. Pies are usually served in the pie plate in which it was baked.

Thermometer

A digital instant-read thermometer that can read up to 200°C is recommended. Some recipes in this book call for mixtures to reach precise temperatures, so having a thermometer is essential when working on those recipes.

Weights

Pie weights are used to blind-bake tart shells and help them retain their shape while baking. Aluminium pie weights are available at baking supply stores, but dried beans work perfectly. Use whatever that is readily available.

Whisk

Choose a stainless-steel whisk with solid and fine wires in a bulbous shape. A whisk with more wires is more efficient. The size of the whisk should correspond to the bowl it is used with. Select a whisk with a nice weight to it, as too light a whisk demands more energy.

Wire Rack

A wire rack or cooling rack allows freshly baked cakes and cookies to cool down efficiently. One that holds your largest baking tin would suffice.

Ingredients

Almond Powder

Almond power, also known as almond flour or almond meal, is made from finely grated blanched almonds. It adds a rich nutty taste to baked goods. Choose finely grated almond powder for the best results.

Baking Powder

Used as a leavening agent in baking. Sift the required amount of baking powder with the other dry ingredients before using to ensure equal distribution.

Butter

Unsalted butter is commonly used for baking because it allows the baker to have more control over the salt content in the baked products. Standard supermarket butter would have 80–81% butterfat content. Keep butter wrapped up in the refrigerator to avoid absorption of refrigerator smells.

Cheese

Cream cheese, mascarpone cheese and hard cheese are used in this book. Whichever brand of cheese you use, be sure to get the full-fat option, or be ready to compromise on the taste and texture of the final product. For hard cheeses, freshly grated is best.

Chocolate

Dark couverture chocolate (58% cocoa) is used in most recipes in this book. Chocolate buttons are preferred in professional kitchens as they are easy to measure, portion and melt down as compared to large slabs of chocolate. Do not store chocolate in the refrigerator because it will absorb moisture and smells. Keep wrapped and store at room temperature.

Cocoa Powder

Cocoa powder is extracted from cocoa beans, leaving behind the fat component which is cocoa butter. In baking, use Dutch-processed (alkalised) unsweetened cocoa powder. Always sift cocoa powder before use.

Eggs

All recipes in this book require large eggs that weigh approximately 60 g with shell. The white should be about 35 g, and the yolk about 20 g. Fresh, free-range eggs are recommended in baking as they help generate more volume when beaten and produce a richer taste. Make a habit of bringing all eggs required in a recipe to room temperature for 30 minutes before using.

Flour

Pastry flour is used in all recipes in this book. It is also known as top flour and is similar to cake flour and Hong Kong flour. These flours have a low protein content which produces light-textured cakes and cookies. All flours must be sifted before using.

Gelatin

Gelatin comes in sheet form and power form and both need to be bloomed. Sheet gelatin is preferred as it is easier to store, measure, bloom and melt. Powdered gelatin needs to be added together with its blooming liquid, which might alter the overall liquid ratio in the recipe. Sheet gelatin must be bloomed in iced water (especially in Singapore's heat) or parts of it will dissolve into the liquid and you will not get the full amount of gelatin required for the recipe. Keep sheet gelatin wrapped up and store in a cool, dry place.

Glucose

Glucose is an invert sugar used in many recipes in this book. It is a thick, clear syrup that adds body to the end product and reduces the chance of crystallisation. Glucose helps cakes remain soft and moist without imparting any flavour of its own and thus does not interfere with other flavours in the recipe. Corn syrup cannot be used as a substitute as it is far sweeter and looser.

Green Tea Powder

Green tea powder or matcha is made from dried and finely ground green tea leaves. 100% pure green tea is preferred but it demands careful storage such as in a dark-coloured bag or container to prolong its shelf life. Pure green tea powder will start to turn dull after light exposure for a day. If it does not, it probably contains green colouring to preserve its appearance.

Gula Melaka

Also known as palm sugar, *gula melaka* has a rich, unique taste that pairs well with coconut and dairy and is widely used in desserts in South East Asia. It is usually sold in discs, so cut and weigh accordingly.

Heavy Cream

Fresh cream is made from milk fat and is used in mousses and for decoration. Try to get cream with more than 35% fat content to produce a silky, light cream when whipped. If required in a recipe here, there is no substitution. Heavy cream cannot be left at room temperature for long periods of time. Store whipped cream in the refrigerator when not in use.

Honey

Honey is a natural sweetener and, unlike glucose, it adds flavour. Choose an all-natural honey and store in a cool place.

Milk

Whole milk is used for all recipes in this book. Avoid low-fat or skim milk, if possible, for the best results.

Nuts

Raw, unsalted almonds, walnuts, hazelnuts, pecans and macadamia are widely used in baking. Store nuts in the refrigerator to extend their shelf-life as their high fat content mean they can go rancid rather quickly. Always taste the nuts before using.

Sugar

White granulated sugar is used in most recipes not just to provide sweetness but also to stabilise the foaming of eggs and to prevent drying. Icing sugar, on the other hand, is used mainly for decoration. Icing sugar contains 1–2% cornflour to prevent clumping, but it can still clump up in Singapore's humidity. Always sift icing sugar if using in batter, and sift it directly onto baked goods if using only for decoration.

Vanilla

Vanilla bean and extract are used in this book. Vanilla beans create a lovely speckled appearance commonly seen in custard creams and crème brûlée, and impart a strong flavour even after heating. If using extract, choose a quality extract. It is often referred to as "bourbon vanilla".

Weights and Measures

Quantities for this book are given in Metric, Imperial and American (spoon) measures. Standard spoon and cup measurements used are: 1 tsp = 5 ml, 1 Tbsp = 15 ml, 1 cup = 250 ml. All measures are level unless otherwise stated.

LIQUID AND VOLUME MEASURES

Metric	Imperial	American
5 ml	$1/6$ fl oz	1 teaspoon
10 ml	$1/3$ fl oz	1 dessertspoon
15 ml	$1/2$ fl oz	1 tablespoon
60 ml	2 fl oz	$1/4$ cup (4 tablespoons)
85 ml	$2^1/2$ fl oz	$1/3$ cup
90 ml	3 fl oz	$3/8$ cup (6 tablespoons)
125 ml	4 fl oz	$1/2$ cup
180 ml	6 fl oz	$3/4$ cup
250 ml	8 fl oz	1 cup
300 ml	10 fl oz ($1/2$ pint)	$1^1/4$ cups
375 ml	12 fl oz	$1^1/2$ cups
435 ml	14 fl oz	$1^3/4$ cups
500 ml	16 fl oz	2 cups
625 ml	20 fl oz (1 pint)	$2^1/2$ cups
750 ml	24 fl oz ($1^1/5$ pints)	3 cups
1 litre	32 fl oz ($1^3/5$ pints)	4 cups
1.25 litres	40 fl oz (2 pints)	5 cups
1.5 litres	48 fl oz ($2^2/5$ pints)	6 cups
2.5 litres	80 fl oz (4 pints)	10 cups

DRY MEASURES

Metric	Imperial
30 grams	1 ounce
45 grams	$1^1/2$ ounces
55 grams	2 ounces
70 grams	$2^1/2$ ounces
85 grams	3 ounces
100 grams	$3^1/2$ ounces
110 grams	4 ounces
125 grams	$4^1/2$ ounces
140 grams	5 ounces
280 grams	10 ounces
450 grams	16 ounces (1 pound)
500 grams	1 pound, $1^1/2$ ounces
700 grams	$1^1/2$ pounds
800 grams	$1^1/2$ pounds
1 kilogram	2 pounds, 3 ounces
1.5 kilograms	3 pounds, $4^1/2$ ounces
2 kilograms	4 pounds, 6 ounces

OVEN TEMPERATURE

	°C	°F	Gas Regulo
Very slow	120	250	1
Slow	150	300	2
Moderately slow	160	325	3
Moderate	180	350	4
Moderately hot	190/200	375/400	5/6
Hot	210/220	410/425	6/7
Very hot	230	450	8
Super hot	250/290	475/550	9/10

LENGTH

Metric	Imperial
0.5 cm	$1/4$ inch
1 cm	$1/2$ inch
1.5 cm	$3/4$ inch
2.5 cm	1 inch

Basic Recipes

CUSTARD CREAM

Makes 350 g cream

This smooth, delicate cream is typically used as a filling for tarts, choux puffs and puff pastry cakes.

Level of Difficulty: Difficult

10 g cornflour

10 g pastry flour

200 g milk

¹/₂ **pod vanilla bean, split**
  lengthwise, seeds scraped

10 g sugar

30 g unsalted butter

7 g salted butter

45 g egg yolks,
  at room temperature

43 g sugar

50 g milk

Chef's Tip

High heat and vigorous whisking are essential for success when making custard cream.

The small amount of sugar added to the milk and butter mixture in the beginning prevents the mixture from burning.

1 Sift together cornflour and pastry flour. Set aside. In a saucepan, simmer 200 g milk, vanilla seeds and pod, 10 g sugar and butters over medium heat until butter is melted and sugar is dissolved. Set aside.

2 In a mixing bowl, whisk egg yolks with 43 g sugar until pale. Add sifted flours and whisk until fully incorporated. Add 50 g milk and mix well. Add mixture from saucepan and mix until uniform.

3 Strain into another saucepan and place over high heat, whisking vigorously until mixture is thickened. The mixture will bubble at the centre throughout. Transfer to a mixing bowl.

4 Prepare a large bowl of iced water and place mixing bowl over it. Using a rubber spatula, scrape base and sides of bowl until custard cream is cold to the touch and the surface is shiny.

5 Cover cream with plastic wrap, pressing down onto surface of cream. Refrigerate for at least 1 hour before using. Custard cream will keep refrigerated for up to 2 days.

PÂTE À CHOUX

Makes 250 g dough or 15 choux puffs, each about 4 cm in diameter

This classic choux recipe is used in many Japanese pastries.

Level of Difficulty: Moderate

72 g pastry flour +
   more for marking

60 g milk

60 g water

60 g unsalted butter

2 g salt

4 g sugar

2 eggs, at room temperature,
   lightly beaten

1 egg white, if needed

Fine mist spray with some
   water

Chef's Tip

If the dough is too hard (step 5), egg white can be added a little at a time to achieve the right consistency. If too much egg white is added and the dough becomes too soft, the dough will need to be discarded and prepared again.

When lowering the oven temperature in step 7, do not be tempted to open the oven door as this will cause the puffs to sink.

Spraying the batter with water creates moisture in the oven, which results in a more tender puff.

1 Preheat oven to 200°C. Line baking trays with parchment paper. Dip a 4-cm round cookie cutter into flour for marking and mark circles 4 cm apart on prepared baking trays. Sift pastry flour.

2 In a saucepan, stir milk, water, unsalted butter, salt and sugar over medium heat until mixture starts to boil. Remove from heat. Whisk in pastry flour until fully incorporated.

3 Return saucepan to medium heat. Using a heatproof rubber spatula, stir until dough starts to stick together and pulls away from sides of saucepan. Transfer dough to a medium bowl.

4 Using a spatula, fold in beaten eggs half portion at a time, ensuring full incorporation after each addition. The dough will be thick and elastic.

5 Test by lifting half of dough with the spatula. It should fall off in 3 seconds. If it does not, mix in 1 Tbsp egg white and test again. Repeat if necessary.

6 Transfer dough to a piping bag fitted with a 1-cm round tip and pipe dough to fill flour circles. Using a fine mist spray, lightly spray puffs with water.

7 Bake for 10–12 minutes until dough rises and expands, then lower oven temperature to 180°C and bake for 15–20 minutes until puffs are golden brown.

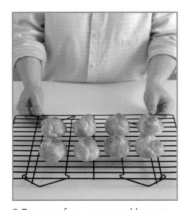

8 Remove from oven and leave to cool on a wire rack before filling puffs. Unfilled choux puffs will keep for up to 1 day in an airtight container.

PÂTE SUCRÉE

Makes 600 g dough, enough for two 18-cm tart bases

This classic sweet tart base has a unique almond flavour.

Level of Difficulty: Easy

200 g pastry flour

50 g bread flour

180 g unsalted butter,
  at room temperature

1/2 tsp salt

95 g sugar

1/2 tsp vanilla extract

1 egg, at room temperature,
  lightly beaten

40 g almond powder

Chef's Tip

If you are preparing this dough ahead of time, you will still need to refrigerate it overnight before placing it into the freezer for storing. This dough can be kept frozen for up to 1 month.

To prevent over mixing, be sure to use a rubber spatula to incorporate the flours and stop as soon as the flours are no longer visible.

1 Sift together pastry flour and bread flour. Set aside. In a large bowl and using a hand whisk, whisk butter, salt, sugar and vanilla extract until smooth and pale.

2 Whisk in beaten egg, half portion at a time, ensuring full incorporation after each addition. Whisk in almond powder, then flour mixture until just combined.

3 Using a rubber spatula, scrape base and sides of bowl until dry ingredients are no longer visible, taking care not to over mix.

4 Place dough on a sheet of plastic wrap and cover tightly. Dough needs to be refrigerated overnight before using.

CRÈME D'AMANDES

Makes 600 g cream

This almond cream is perfect when used in tarts made with pâte sucrée (page 32) or kneaded dough (page 42) as it elevates the overall flavour of the pastry. Simply pipe it into a tart base and bake for 20–25 minutes until golden brown.

Level of Difficulty: Easy

180 g almond powder

1 tsp milk powder

90 g eggs, at room
temperature

2 egg yolks, at room
temperature

160 g unsalted butter,
at room temperature

1/2 tsp vanilla extract

140 g sugar

Chef's Tip

If you are preparing this cream ahead of time, you will still need to refrigerate it overnight before placing it into the freezer for storing. This cream can be kept frozen for up to 1 month.

After adding the sugar and butter, be careful not to over mix or the texture of the cream will be affected.

1 Sift together almond and milk powders. Set aside. Lightly beat together eggs and egg yolks. Set aside. In a large bowl, whisk butter, vanilla extract and sugar until smooth and pale.

2 Add beaten eggs, a third at a time, ensuring full incorporation after each addition. Using a rubber spatula, fold in dry ingredients until mixture is uniform. Do not over mix.

3 Leave **cream** in bowl and cover tightly with plastic wrap, pressing plastic wrap down onto **cream**. Refrigerate overnight before using.

ROLL SPONGE

Makes one 30-cm square sponge

This delicate, soft sponge is perfect for making roll cakes.

Level of Difficulty: Moderate

6 eggs, at room temperature

190 g sugar

75 g milk

38 g unsalted butter

145 g pastry flour, sifted

Chef's Tip

If not using immediately, cover sponge tightly with plastic wrap. This sponge will keep refrigerated for up to 1 day.

When smoothing out the surface of the batter, be sure to do so very gently, and ensure that the batter is of a uniform height, especially at the sides. Clean the flat scraper at the side of the tray and scrape away any batter clinging to the side of the tray to prevent it from burning.

1 Preheat oven to 180°C. Line a shallow 30-cm square baking tray with parchment paper, leaving a 2-cm overhang. Set aside. Fill a pot with water up to 4 cm high and simmer over medium heat.

2 In a heatproof bowl, whisk eggs and sugar lightly. Place bowl over pot of simmering water and whisk constantly in large strokes until mixture reaches 40°C. Transfer to the bowl of a stand mixer.

3 Whisk warm egg mixture at high speed until mixture doubles in volume and turns very pale. Meanwhile, in a saucepan over medium heat, heat milk and butter to 80°C and remove from heat.

4 When egg mixture is ready, turn mixer speed to low. Add warm milk and butter mixture. Beat for 5 seconds, then increase speed to high and beat until mixture is uniform.

5 Switch to using a rubber spatula and fold in sifted flour until fully incorporated. Scrape base and sides of mixing bowl thoroughly. Be careful not to over mix.

6 Pour batter into prepared baking tray. Using a flat scraper, gently smoothen surface of batter in one direction. Bake for 10–12 minutes or until surface of sponge is brown.

7 Test if sponge is done by pressing the centre lightly. It should spring back. Place sponge on a wire rack. Peel away paper at the side. Leave to cool for about 30 minutes.

8 To peel off parchment paper at bottom of sponge, place a cutting board over the sponge and flip it over. Peel off paper and flip sponge back upright. The roll is now ready for use.

SPONGE

Makes one 21-cm round cake

This soft, springy sponge is used as a base for many celebration cakes.
It is also required in some tart and pie recipes in this book.

Level of Difficulty: Easy

25 g unsalted butter

40 g milk

300 g eggs (about 6 eggs),
    at room temperature

170 g sugar

16 g honey

16 g glucose

170 g pastry flour, sifted

Chef's Tip

Be careful not to over mix the batter
after adding the butter or it will
deflate, resulting in a stiff sponge.

An alternative way of testing if the
cake is done is by observing the
parchment paper. It will shrink away
from the sides of the baking tin when
the cake is baked and ready.

1 Preheat oven to 180°C. Line a 21-cm round baking tin with parchment paper, leaving a 2-cm overhang. Simmer butter and milk until butter is melted. Remove from heat.

2 Fill a pot with water up to 4 cm high and simmer over medium heat. In a heatproof bowl, lightly whisk eggs, sugar, honey and glucose.

3 Place bowl over pot of simmering water and whisk constantly in large strokes until mixture is warm, about 40°C. Transfer to the mixing bowl of a stand mixer.

4 Using a stand mixer, whisk mixture at high speed until tripled in volume and very pale. Use the whisk to draw a ribbon in the batter. The shape should not dissolve immediately.

5 Using a spatula, fold in flour, a third at a time, ensuring full incorporation after each addition. Turn the bowl as you fold the flour in, and scrape base and sides of bowl well.

6 Using a rubber spatula and mixing in a circular motion, mix in warm milk and butter mixture. Mix thoroughly, scraping base and sides of bowl. Stop as soon as mixture is even.

7 Pour batter into prepared baking tin and bake for 35–40 minutes, until top of cake is golden brown and a skewer inserted into the centre of cake comes out clean.

8 Unmould sponge and place on a wire rack to cool for about 30 minutes before peeling off parchment paper. Sponge is now ready for use.

BISCUITS À LA CUILLÈRE

Makes about 30 fingers

Commonly known as ladyfingers, these biscuits are often used in making the Italian dessert, tiramisu, as well as to line decoration cakes.

Level of Difficulty: Easy

78 g egg yolks,
  at room temperature

26 g icing sugar +
  more for dusting

120 g pastry flour, sifted

MERINGUE

140 g egg whites,
  at room temperature

104 g sugar

Chef's Tip

This recipe is sufficient for lining the sides of two 18-cm round cakes. Any excess is delicious eaten on its own.

Watch the baking time and be careful not to over bake these biscuits.

1 Preheat oven to 200°C. Line 2 baking trays with parchment paper. Prepare meringue. Using a handheld mixer at high speed, whisk egg whites and one-third of sugar for 1¹/₂ minutes.

2 Add another one-third of sugar and whisk for another 1 minute. Add remaining sugar and whisk for another 2 minutes until meringue is glossy and forms soft peaks. Set aside.

3 In another bowl, whisk egg yolks and 26 g icing sugar until pale. Add one-third of meringue and whisk until just incorporated. Switch to a rubber spatula and fold in remaining meringue.

4 Fold in pastry flour, one-third portion at a time, ensuring full incorporation after each addition. Stop mixing as soon as flour is no longer visible. Be careful not to over mix.

5 Transfer mixture to a piping bag fitted with a 1.5-cm round tip. Pipe 7-cm long lines on trays, spacing them 3 cm apart. Dust well with icing sugar and let rest for 1–2 minutes, then dust again lightly.

6 Bake for 10–12 minutes until cracks start to appear on the surface of biscuits and they are hard on the outside. Remove from oven and transfer to a wire rack to cool. Consume within the day.

KNEADED DOUGH

Makes 580 g dough, enough for an 18-cm round crust

This recipe uses a method that is very popular in Japan for making a buttery, flaky pastry similar to puff pastry.

Level of Difficulty: Difficult

110 g milk, chilled

4 g salt

133 g bread flour, chilled

92 g pastry flour, chilled + more for dusting

250 g unsalted butter, cut into small cubes and frozen overnight

Chef's Tip

In hot and humid weather, roll out the dough at night when it is cooler or in an air-conditioned room.

As this dough is very buttery, it is likely to soften and stick to the work surface when rolling out. If this happens, lightly dust the work surface with flour before rolling again. Alternatively, return the dough to the refrigerator for 15 minutes before working on it again.

1 Mix milk and salt in a cup. Sift together bread and pastry flours into the bowl of a stand mixer fitted with a paddle attachment. Add frozen butter and beat at low speed for 10 seconds.

2 Add milk and salt mixture and beat until dough just barely starts to stick to the paddle and flour is no longer visible. The dough will be crumbly with bits of butter still visible.

3 Place dough on a sheet of plastic wrap and press it together to form a compressed disc. Cover tightly with plastic wrap and keep refrigerated overnight.

4 Lightly dust a work surface with flour and roll out dough into a 50 x 20-cm rectangle. If dough starts to get sticky, dust lightly with flour before rolling again.

5 Fold dough into thirds and roll out again into a rectangle. If dough starts to get sticky, dust lightly with flour or refrigerate for about 15 minutes for it to firm up.

6 Repeat to fold and roll dough another 2 times. If dough starts to get sticky, dust lightly with flour or refrigerate for about 15 minutes for it to firm up.

7 Cover with plastic wrap and refrigerate for at least 2 hours before repeating to roll and fold chilled dough another 4 times.

8 If not using immediately, cover dough with plastic wrap and store refrigerated for up to 3 days or freeze for up to 1 week.

Cookies

DACQUOISE AUX RAISINS

Makes about 16 cookies

This meringue-based cookie is crunchy on the outside and soft on the inside. It is usually sandwiched together with cream or jam.

Level of Difficulty: Moderate

10 g pastry flour + more
  for dusting

60 g almond powder

60 g icing sugar + more
  for dusting

250 g pâte sucrée dough
  (page 32)

250 g dried mixed fruit
  with rum (available from
  baking supply stores)

100 g egg whites, at room
  temperature

30 g sugar

Chef's Tip

The process of heating the egg white and sugar mixture (step 4) cannot be skipped as it is an essential step for a successful meringue.

The desirable crunchy exterior of the meringue is created by coating it twice with icing sugar before baking.

1 Preheat oven to 180°C. Line baking trays with parchment paper. Sift together pastry flour, almond powder and icing sugar onto a sheet of parchment paper. Set aside.

2 Dust a work surface and roll out pâte sucrée dough into a 0.3-cm thick sheet. Using a 5-cm round cookie cutter, cut out 16 rounds of dough. Place on prepared baking trays, spacing them 3 cm apart.

6 Using a rubber spatula, fold sifted pastry flour, almond powder and icing sugar into meringue until flour is no longer visible. Take care not to deflate meringue.

7 Transfer meringue into a piping bag fitted with a 1.5-cm round tip. Pipe meringue onto dough rounds starting from outside in to cover dried fruit.

3 Prick dough rounds all over with a fork and place a teaspoon of dried fruit on each round. Set aside. Fill a pot with water up to 4 cm high and simmer over medium heat.

4 In a heatproof bowl, combine egg whites and one-third of sugar. Place bowl over pot of simmering water and whisk slowly until mixture reaches 40°C. Remove from heat.

5 Using a handheld mixer, whisk warmed egg whites at high speed until soft foam forms. Add remaining two-thirds sugar and continue whisking at high speed until there is no more liquid.

8 Finish by piping a small dome at the centre. Dust meringue well with icing sugar and let rest for 1–2 minutes, then dust again lightly.

9 Bake for 17–20 minutes or until meringue is lightly browned and surface is cracked. Leave to cool on a wire rack. Store in an airtight container for up to 2 days.

GALETTE BRETONNE

Makes 24 cookies

This cookie has its roots in Brittany, France. Because of its buttery nature, it is best that all the ingredients are prepared beforehand so the cookie can be made quickly before the butter melts.

Level of Difficulty: Moderate

- 300 g pastry flour + more for dusting
- ½ tsp baking powder
- 1 egg, at room temperature
- 2 egg yolks, at room temperature
- 100 g dried mixed fruit with rum (available from baking supply stores)
- 25 g rum

- 250 g salted butter, at room temperature
- 150 g icing sugar, sifted
- 85 g almond powder, sifted

EGG WASH
- 1 egg yolk
- 10 g milk
- ½ tsp honey

Chef's Tip

When broken into two, a perfect galette is pale in the centre and golden brown on the outside.

1 Sift together pastry flour and baking powder. Set aside. In a bowl, lightly beat egg and egg yolks. In another bowl, combine dried fruit and rum. Leave for 10 minutes.

2 Using a stand mixer, beat butter until light and creamy. Add icing sugar and beat until mixture turns pale. Add almond powder and beat until incorporated.

3 Add beaten eggs, half portion at a time, until fully incorporated. Switch to a rubber spatula and fold in dried fruit with rum. Add flour and fold in until just uniform.

4 Dust a work surface with flour and knead dough lightly. Roll it out into a 1.2-cm thick sheet, then cover and refrigerate for at least 30 minutes until firm. Combine ingredients for egg wash in a bowl.

5 Unwrap chilled dough and place on a sheet of parchment paper. Using a 6-cm round cookie cutter, cut out 24 rounds of dough. Brush surface of dough rounds lightly with egg wash.

6 Place dough rounds into aluminium cups on baking trays. Using the prongs of a fork, score the surface of each round to create a pattern. Bake for 30–35 minutes until cookies are golden brown.

7 Remove from oven and leave to cool on a wire rack before serving or storing. These cookies will keep in an airtight container for up to 4 days.

FLORENTINES

Makes 20 cookies

These pretty Italian cookies are made using pâte sucrée for the base and topped with nougatine.

Level of Difficulty: Moderate

**Melted butter for
  greasing moulds**

Flour for dusting

**300 g pâte sucrée dough
  (page 32)**

125 g raw sliced almonds

12 g pastry flour

85 g heavy cream

110 g sugar

50 g unsalted butter

25 g honey

25 g glucose

 Chef's Tip

It is important that raw almonds are used in this recipe as almonds that are already baked will brown too much when baked again.

You will need to use a candy thermometer when preparing these cookies to ensure that the nougat is not overheated.

1 Preheat oven to 180°C. Lightly grease 20 small tart tins, each 6 x 2-cm, with melted butter. Dust a work surface with flour and roll out pâte sucrée dough into a 0.4-cm thick sheet.

2 Using a 5-cm round cookie cutter, cut out 20 rounds of dough and place into buttered tart tins. Prick dough all over with a fork. Arrange tart tins on 2 baking trays.

3 Bake for 10 minutes or until dough starts to brown. Remove from oven and set aside. Keep oven heated. In a bowl, mix sliced almonds with pastry flour. Set aside.

4 Place heavy cream, sugar, unsalted butter, honey and glucose in a pan over medium heat. Mix with a wooden spoon until mixture reaches 105°C. Remove from heat.

5 Add almond slices and mix until combined. Set aside to cool for 5 minutes. Using a tablespoon, spoon mixture into moulds over pâte sucrée rounds.

6 Bake for 18–20 minutes, or until nougat is rich brown in colour. Leave to cool before unmoulding. These cookies will keep in an airtight container for up to 4 days.

CAYENNE PEPPER COOKIES

Makes about 30 cookies

These sweet and slightly spicy cookies are lightly flavoured with cheese.

Level of Difficulty: Easy

180 g pastry flour

4 g salt

2 g cayenne pepper

1 g hot paprika

1 egg, at room temperature

1 egg yolk, at room temperature

180 g unsalted butter, at room temperature

135 g sugar

220 g edam or gruyére cheese, finely grated

90 g almond powder

 Chef's Tip

Be careful not to over mix the batter or the cookies will be hard.

1 Preheat oven to 160°C. Line 2–3 baking trays with parchment paper. Sift together pastry flour, salt, cayenne pepper and hot paprika. Set aside. Beat egg and egg yolk together lightly. Set aside.

2 Using a stand mixer, beat butter and sugar at high speed until mixture is pale. Add cheese and almond powder and mix at medium speed. Add eggs and continue to mix at medium speed.

3 Add flour mixture and beat at low speed until well mixed. Transfer batter to a piping bag fitted with a 2-cm basket weave tip. Pipe long strips of dough onto prepared trays.

4 Bake for 12–15 minutes or until cookies are golden brown. While still hot, cut cookies into 4-cm lengths. Leave to cool. Keep in an airtight container for up to 1 week.

TUILES AUX AMANDES

Makes about 15 cookies

These thin, fragrant almond cookies can be enjoyed on their own or served as a garnish on desserts.

Level of Difficulty: Easy

30 g egg white,
  at room temperature

50 g sugar

100 g raw sliced almonds

15 g pastry flour

15 g unsalted butter, melted

 Chef's Tip

Leaving the dough to sit at room temperature for 30–60 minutes (step 3) will allow the ingredients to meld and form a mixture that is easy to spread.

When shaping the cookies into domes, you can also use a wine bottle or cup. While shaping one tray of cookies, leave the other tray in the oven (with the power turned off) to keep the unshaped cookies warm and malleable. You will not be able to shape them once they have cooled.

1 Fill a pot with water up to 4 cm high and simmer over medium heat. Place egg white and sugar in a heatproof bowl and whisk slowly over simmering water until mixture reaches 40°C. Remove from heat.

2 In a bowl, mix sliced almonds with pastry flour. Using a rubber spatula, fold almond slices gently into whisked egg white. Add warm melted butter and mix until combined.

3 Cover bowl with plastic wrap and leave dough to rest at room temperature for 30–60 minutes. When dough is ready, preheat oven to 180°C. Line baking trays with parchment paper.

4 Using a fork dipped first in water, drop a spoonful of batter onto baking tray, then spread it out into a 7-cm round. Repeat to make more tuiles, spacing them 3 cm apart.

5 Bake for 12–13 minutes until golden brown. Using a metal spatula, lift cookies while they are still hot and drape them over a wooden rolling pin to shape them.

6 Leave cookies on the rolling pin for 1 minute before removing to a wire rack to cool completely. These cookies will keep in an airtight container for up to 3 days.

Tea Cakes

Bouchée 60

Coconut Gula Melaka Madeleines 64

Brownie 66

Hoji-cha Butter Castellas 68

BOUCHÉE

Makes about 20

This meringue-based sandwich cake is crisp on the outside and soft on the inside.

Level of Difficulty: Difficult

CREAM FILLING

100 g heavy cream

7 g sugar

250 g custard cream
(page 28)

BATTER

60 g almond powder

60 g bread flour

$^1/_2$ tsp baking powder

80 g eggs, at room
temperature, lightly beaten

60 g sugar

90 g egg yolks, at room
temperature

MERINGUE

160 g egg whites

60 g sugar

Icing sugar for dusting

Chef's Tip

When adding the meringue to the batter, work quickly and be careful not to over mix or the batter will deflate and the cakes will not rise.

1 Prepare cream filling. Using a handheld mixer, whisk heavy cream and sugar until soft peaks form. Switch to a rubber spatula and fold in custard cream. Cover with plastic wrap and keep refrigerated.

2 Prepare batter. Sift almond powder, bread flour and baking powder into a large bowl. Using a rubber spatula, fold beaten eggs into sifted ingredients, half portion at a time.

6 Add another one-third of sugar and whisk until meringue is voluminous. Add remaining portion of sugar and whisk until meringue is glossy and forms stiff peaks.

7 Using a rubber spatula, work quickly to fold half the meringue into batter, being careful not to deflate meringue. Repeat with remaining half of meringue.

3 Add sugar, half portion at a time, ensuring full incorporation after each addition. Scrape bowl thoroughly. Using a hand whisk, whisk in egg yolks in three additions, mixing well each time.

4 Switch to a rubber spatula and fold batter with quick and big strokes until it lightens in colour. Set aside. Preheat oven to 180°C and line 2 baking trays with parchment paper.

5 Prepare meringue. Using a handheld mixer at high speed, whisk egg whites until foamy. Add one-third of sugar and whisk until egg whites are no longer liquid.

8 Transfer mixture to a piping bag fitted with a 1.2-cm round tip. Pipe domes about 4 cm in diameter onto prepared baking trays, spacing them 3 cm apart.

9 Dust well with icing sugar and let rest for 1–2 minutes before dusting again lightly. Bake for 25–27 minutes, until meringue is cracked and they are hard on the outside.

10 Leave meringues on parchment paper and place on wire racks to cool. When cool, sandwich meringues with cream filling. Consume immediately or refrigerate for up to 1 day.

COCONUT GULA MELAKA MADELEINES

Makes about 18 madeleines

This recipe infuses South East Asian flavours into the French tea cake with the addition of *gula melaka*, a palm sugar with a distinctive taste.

Level of Difficulty: Easy

Melted unsalted butter for greasing mould

120 g pastry flour

2 g baking powder

15 g almond powder

5 g cornflour

7 g milk powder

35 g desiccated coconut

17 g honey

46 g heavy cream

46 g salted butter

46 g unsalted butter

70 g *gula melaka* (palm sugar), roughly chopped

2 eggs, at room temperature

2 egg yolks, at room temperature

80 g brown sugar

 Chef's Tip

In this recipe, the butter is added to the batter last, which gives these tea cakes a rich buttery flavour and soft texture.

1 Preheat oven to 170°C. Lightly grease a madeleine mould with melted unsalted butter. Sift together pastry flour, baking powder, almond powder, cornflour and milk powder. Whisk in desiccated coconut. Set aside.

2 Combine honey, heavy cream, both types of butter and *gula melaka* in a saucepan over medium heat. Using a wooden spoon, stir until butter and sugar are melted and mixture reaches 80°C. Set aside.

3 Using a handheld mixer, whisk eggs, egg yolks and brown sugar at high speed for 3 minutes until mixture doubles in volume and is pale. Using a rubber spatula, fold in dry ingredients.

4 Lastly, fold in warm butter mixture. Scrape base and sides of bowl thoroughly. Pour batter into prepared mould and bake for 20–25 minutes or until top of cakes are golden brown.

5 Remove from oven. Unmould cakes and leave on a wire rack to cool before serving or storing. These cakes will keep refrigerated in an airtight container for up to 3 days.

BROWNIE

Makes one 24-cm square cake

This rich American chocolate cake will
be a favourite with chocolate lovers.

Level of Difficulty: Easy

Melted butter for
  greasing mould

230 g unsalted butter,
  at room temperature

113 g dark chocolate
  buttons (58% cocoa)

320 g sugar

4 eggs, at room temperature

1 tsp vanilla extract

110 g pastry flour, sifted

125 g walnuts, roughly
  chopped

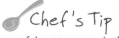 Chef's Tip

Be careful not to over mix the
batter after adding the flour
(step 3) or the texture of the
cake will be hard.

1 Preheat oven to 160°C. Lightly
grease a 24-cm square baking tin
with melted butter, then line base
with parchment paper. Fill a pot
with water up to 4 cm high and
simmer over medium heat.

2 Place butter and chocolate
buttons into a heatproof bowl
over simmering water and stir with
a rubber spatula until mixture is
melted and well mixed. Remove
from heat.

3 Add sugar and mix until
dissolved. Add eggs, two at
a time, mixing well after each
addition. Stir in vanilla extract.
Fold in pastry flour until flour is no
longer visible. Do not over mix.

4 Fold in chopped walnuts and
pour batter into prepared tin.
Bake for 30 minutes or until a
skewer inserted into the centre of
cake comes out clean. Remove
from oven.

5 Leave cake to cool slightly
before unmoulding. Place on
a wire rack to cool completely.
Slice to serve. This brownie will
keep refrigerated in an airtight
container for up to 3 days.

HOJI-CHA BUTTER CASTELLAS

Makes two 15-cm round cakes

Hoji-cha is an aromatic roasted green tea. In this recipe, it is used to flavour a simple Japanese sponge cake.

Level of Difficulty: Easy

**Melted butter for
  greasing moulds**

Bread flour for coating mould

240 g eggs, at room temperature

200 g sugar

50 g glucose

15 g honey

10 g water

**12 g *hoji-cha*, blended
  into a powder**

125 g pastry flour

125 g unsalted butter

Icing sugar for dusting

 *Chef's Tip*

Be careful not to over mix the batter after adding the flour or the texture of the cake will be affected.

Hoji-cha can be substituted with any tea of choice.

1 Preheat oven to 180°C. Lightly grease the sides of two 15-cm round baking tins with melted butter, then coat with bread flour, tapping out any excess flour. Line base of tins with 2 layers of parchment paper.

2 Fill a pot with water up to 4 cm high and simmer over medium heat. In a heatproof bowl, combine eggs and sugar. Place over simmering water and whisk until mixture reaches 45°C.

3 Remove bowl from heat. Using a handheld mixer, whisk mixture at high speed until very smooth. Test consistency by drawing a ribbon in batter. The ribbon should disappear in 1–2 seconds. Set aside.

4 In a saucepan over medium heat, stir glucose, honey and water together until even. In another saucepan, heat butter until simmering. Remove from heat. Sift together *hoji-cha* powder and flour.

5 Using a rubber spatula, fold glucose mixture into batter until combined. Fold in *hoji-cha* and flour mixture, then fold in melted butter. Scrape base and sides of bowl thoroughly.

6 Divide batter between prepared moulds. Bake for 28–30 minutes or until cakes are golden brown and a skewer inserted into the centre of cakes comes out clean. Remove from oven.

7 Leave cakes to cool slightly before unmoulding. Place on a wire rack to cool completely. Dust with icing sugar before serving. Store in an airtight container in the refrigerator for up to 2 days.

Pies and Tarts

APPLE PIE

Makes one 15-cm round pie

The unique feature of this pie is the sponge which helps absorb the juices from the filling, keeping the pie crust crisp.

Level of Difficulty: Difficult

3 large apples

30 g unsalted butter

30 g brown sugar

3 g ground cinnamon

¹/₃ pod vanilla bean, split lengthwise, seeds scraped

300 g kneaded dough (page 42)

Flour for dusting

1 round sponge (page 38), 15 x 1-cm

1 egg, lightly beaten

 *Chef's Tip*

Due to its high butter content, kneaded dough tends to soften quickly at room temperature. If the dough starts to get sticky as you are working on it, return it to the refrigerator to chill and firm up before rolling out.

1 Cut apples into wedges, then cut away core and skin. Cut into small pieces and set aside. Stir butter, sugar and cinnamon in a saucepan over medium heat until butter is melted.

2 Add apples and vanilla seeds. Cook, stirring, for 10–15 minutes until apples are brown and soft. Leave to cool. Preheat oven to 180°C. Prepare a 15-cm pie plate.

4 Place dough round into pie plate and press it lightly into the edges. Place sponge round over dough. Keep refrigerated until needed.

5 Dust a work surface with flour and roll out other half of dough into a 27 x 20-cm sheet. Cut into 18 strips, each 20 cm long and 1.5 cm wide. Keep refrigerated.

6 Remove pie plate from refrigerator. Drain apples, then spoon them on top of sponge round. Level out the apples and space them out evenly.

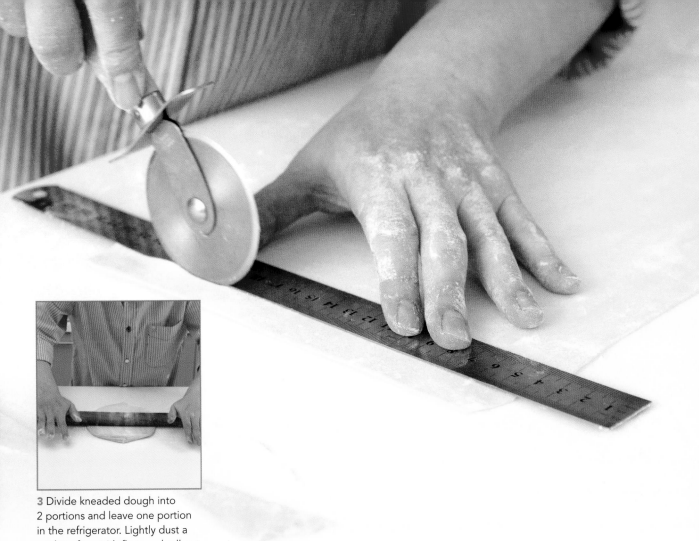

3 Divide kneaded dough into 2 portions and leave one portion in the refrigerator. Lightly dust a work surface with flour and roll out kneaded dough into a round about 25 cm in diameter.

7 Lightly brush edges of dough lining pie plate with beaten egg. Place 8 dough strips over filling, spacing them 1 cm apart. Brush with beaten egg, then place 8 strips across in a trellis pattern. Trim off excess dough.

8 Lightly brush circumference of pie with beaten egg and make trimming with remaining 2 dough strips, pressing them lightly to adhere. Brush dough lightly with beaten egg.

9 Bake for 40–45 minutes until top of pie is golden brown. Remove from oven and leave to cool before cutting and serving. This pie will keep refrigerated for up to 2 days.

PUMPKIN PIE

Makes one 15-cm round pie

This pumpkin pie is free from spices, which allows the natural sweetness of the pumpkin to come through.

Level of Difficulty: Difficult

450 g kneaded dough (page 42), chilled

Flour for dusting

1 round sponge, 15 x 1-cm (page 38)

1 egg, lightly beaten

PUMPKIN FILLING

126 g sugar

30 g unsalted butter

36 g heavy cream

400 g canned pumpkin purée

1 egg, lightly beaten

Chef's Tip

Keep kneaded dough refrigerated when not using as the high fat content causes it to soften easily.

Make your own pumpkin purée by slicing a Japanese pumpkin into wedges, scraping out the seeds and steaming it until soft. Remove the skin and mash finely.

1 Divide kneaded dough into 2 portions and leave one portion in the refrigerator. Lightly dust a work surface with flour and roll out kneaded dough into a round, about 25 cm in diameter.

2 Place dough round into a 15-cm pie plate and press it lightly into the edges. Trim off any excess dough. Place sponge round over dough. Keep refrigerated until needed.

6 Preheat oven to 180°C. Roll out other half of kneaded dough into a round about 25 cm in diameter. Set aside. Remove pie plate from refrigerator and spoon pumpkin filling over sponge.

7 Lightly brush edges of dough lining pie plate with beaten egg, then place dough round over to cover filling, pressing edges firmly to seal. Lightly brush top of pie with beaten egg.

3 Prepare pumpkin filling. In a pan over medium heat, bring sugar, butter and heavy cream to a simmer, stirring constantly to prevent burning. Add pumpkin purée and mix well.

4 Cook for 4 minutes, stirring constantly to prevent burning. Remove pan from heat. Add beaten egg, half portion at a time, mixing thoroughly after each addition.

5 Once egg is fully incorporated, return to medium heat, stirring constantly, for another 3 minutes. Transfer pumpkin filling to a bowl, cover and refrigerate for 30 minutes.

8 Fold and press edges of dough in at about 5-cm intervals to create a floral pattern. Then, using a skewer, score the dough with curved lines, starting from the centre of the pie, to complete the floral pattern.

9 Bake for 35–45 minutes, or until crust is golden. Remove from oven and place on a wire rack. Leave to cool completely before serving. Store refrigerated for up to 2 days.

STRAWBERRY MILLEFEUILLE

Makes one 25 x 12.5-cm pastry

This popular Japanese confection is made with crisp puff pastry and flavoured with Chantilly cream. It is best served immediately.

Level of Difficulty: Difficult

Flour for dusting

300 g kneaded dough
(page 42), chilled

100 g custard cream
(page 28)

100 g heavy cream

450 g strawberries,
hulled and sliced

Icing sugar for dusting

CHANTILLY CREAM

200 g heavy cream

15 g icing sugar

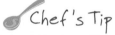 Chef's Tip

Work quickly when rolling out the kneaded dough as this buttery dough is very sensitive to heat. If it starts to stick, dust the work surface with more flour, or refrigerate to firm dough before rolling it out again.

1 Lightly dust a work surface with flour and roll out kneaded dough into a 25-cm square sheet about 0.3-cm thick. Cover dough with plastic wrap and refrigerate for 1 hour.

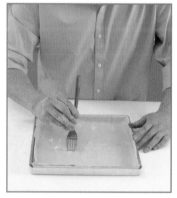

2 Preheat oven to 200°C. Line a 25-cm square baking tray with parchment paper. Remove chilled dough and unwrap. Place into prepared baking tray and prick well with a fork.

6 Pipe some of the cream in straight lines to cover one puff pastry rectangle. Arrange strawberries neatly on top of cream in 3 rows.

7 Pipe more cream over the layer of strawberries, then use a metal spatula to spread cream around the strawberries and to fill up any gaps.

8 Sandwich with the other puff pastry rectangle, keeping the smooth side of the pastry facing up. Refrigerate pastry for 1 hour or until cream is set.

3 Bake for 35–40 minutes, or until pastry is puffed and golden brown. Remove from oven and set aside to cool. Meanwhile, in a medium bowl and using a hand whisk, whisk custard cream until smooth.

4 In another bowl and using a handheld mixer, whisk heavy cream at high speed until soft peaks form. Using a rubber spatula, fold whipped cream into custard cream until well mixed. Keep refrigerated.

5 Cut cooled puff pastry into two equal rectangles. Trim the edges, then crush trimmed edges in a bowl. Set aside. Transfer cream to a piping bag fitted with a 0.8-cm round tip.

9 Prepare Chantilly cream. Place heavy cream and icing sugar in a bowl set over a larger bowl of iced water. Using a handheld mixer, whisk at high speed until stiff peaks form.

10 Transfer cream to a piping bag fitted with a 0.8-cm round tip. Pipe some cream around sides of pastry and spread with a spatula. Press pastry crumbs into the sides to coat.

11 Pipe cream over top of pastry and decorate with remaining strawberries. Dust with icing sugar and serve immediately as this pastry does not keep well.

TARTE AU FROMAGE

Makes one 18-cm round tart

This baked cheese tart is light and creamy with a hint of lemon.

Level of Difficulty: Easy

180 g cream cheese,
  at room temperature

20 g sour cream,
  at room temperature

2 egg yolks, at room
  temperature

15 g pastry flour, sifted

$\frac{1}{2}$ lemon, grated for zest
  and squeezed for 10 g juice

18-cm round pâte sucrée
  tart base, blind-baked for
  20–25 minutes (page 86)

MERINGUE

40 g egg whites

35 g sugar

1 Preheat oven to 150°C. Using a handheld mixer, whisk cream cheese and sour cream at low speed until smooth. Add egg yolks and mix well.

2 Using a rubber spatula, fold flour into cream cheese mixture until flour is no longer visible. Fold in lemon zest and juice. Scrape base and sides of bowl well. Set aside.

3 Prepare meringue. Using a handheld mixer, whisk egg whites and sugar, starting at low speed and gradually increasing to high speed until mixture is white and still runny.

4 Using a rubber spatula, fold meringue, half portion at a time, into cream cheese mixture until fully incorporated. Be careful not to deflate meringue.

5 Pour mixture into partially baked tart shell and smoothen surface with an offset spatula. Bake for 20–25 minutes, or until surface starts to brown.

6 Remove from oven and leave to cool for 15 minutes. Refrigerate for at least 2 hours before slicing to serve. Store refrigerated for up to 2 days.

TARTE AU CITRON

Makes one 18-cm round tart

This lemon tart features a silky lemon meringue atop a sweet tart base with a unique almond flavour.

Level of Difficulty: Difficult

Flour for dusting

300 g pâte sucrée dough (page 32)

1 round sponge, 18 x 0.5-cm (page 38) or slices of sandwich bread

Icing sugar for dusting

LEMON CURD

192 g eggs

140 g sugar

100 g sour cream

1¹/₂ lemons, grated for zest and squeezed for 50 g juice

ITALIAN MERINGUE

80 g sugar

30 g lemon juice

80 g egg whites

20 g sugar

1 Dust a work surface with flour and roll dough into a 0.4-cm thick sheet. Cut out a round using a 21-cm cake ring and press into an 18-cm tart tin. Refrigerate for 30 minutes.

2 Preheat oven to 200°C. Remove tart tin from refrigerator and cover base of dough with parchment paper trimmed to size. Fill tin with dried beans or pie weights.

6 Place pan over low heat, stirring constantly with a rubber spatula until mixture starts to thicken and tiny bubbles form at the sides. Remove pan from heat.

7 Pour lemon curd into baked and cooled tart shell and smoothen the surface using an offset spatula. Top with sponge round or slices of bread and refrigerate.

8 Prepare Italian meringue. In a saucepan, combine 80 g sugar and lemon juice until syrup reaches 118°C. Meanwhile, using a stand mixer, whisk egg whites and 20 g sugar at high speed until foamy.

3 Bake for 20–25 minutes, or until rim of tart shell starts to brown. Remove parchment paper and beans or pie weights, and continue baking tart shell for 10–12 minutes until golden brown.

4 Remove tart shell from oven and leave to cool. Prepare lemon curd. In a large bowl, lightly whisk together eggs and sugar. In a small bowl, lightly whisk sour cream until smooth.

5 Add whisked sour cream to egg and sugar mixture and whisk until fully incorporated. Whisk in lemon juice. Strain mixture into a large pan, then stir in lemon zest.

9 With mixer still beating at high speed, pour hot syrup in a thin stream into foamy egg whites and continue whisking until bowl is cool to the touch and meringue is stiff and glossy.

10 Transfer meringue to a piping bag fitted with a 1-cm round tip. Pipe meringue over top of sponge or bread slices to decorate. Dust meringue lightly with icing sugar.

11 Using a cook's blow torch, lightly brown meringue to create a golden brown finish. Slice to serve. This tart does not keep well and must be consumed within the day.

LA FRANCE

Makes one 18-cm round tart

This classic tart features a creamy custard filling with slices of pear and a sweet pastry crust.

Level of Difficulty: Moderate

Flour for dusting

300 g pâte sucrée dough (page 32)

5 canned pear halves, drained and thinly sliced without cutting through

CUSTARD FILLING

3 eggs

90 g sugar

300 g heavy cream

20 g milk

✎ Chef's Tip

Do not attempt to remove the tart from the tart tin while it is still hot as it may crumble. Leave the tart to cool completely before unmoulding.

1 Dust a work surface with flour and roll dough into a 0.6-cm thick sheet. Cut out a round using a 21-cm cake ring and press into an 18-cm tart tin. Refrigerate for 30 minutes.

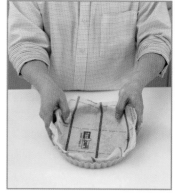

2 Preheat oven to 200°C. Remove tart tin from refrigerator and cover base of dough with parchment paper trimmed to size. Fill tin with dried beans or pie weights.

3 Bake for 40–45 minutes, or until rim of tart shell starts to brown. Remove from oven and leave to cool. Remove parchment paper and beans or pie weights. Lower oven temperature to 160°C.

4 Prepare custard filling. In a medium bowl, lightly whisk eggs to mix. Add sugar and continue to whisk until sugar is dissolved. Add heavy cream and milk and whisk until mixture is uniform.

5 Arrange sliced pear halves in a layer on baked and cooled tart shell. Pour over custard filling and spread evenly. Bake for 35–40 minutes or until filling is set. Remove from oven.

6 Leave tart in tin and place on a wire rack to cool for 15 minutes, before refrigerating for at least 2 hours. Serve chilled. This tart can be kept refrigerated for up to 2 days.

Mousses, Puddings and Jellies

GRAPEFRUIT JELLY

Makes 4 servings

Flavoured with grapefruit juice and lemon juice, this refreshing jelly is set in pretty cups made from grapefruit.

Level of Difficulty: Easy

12 g gelatin sheet
2 medium ruby grapefruit
30 g lemon juice
120 g sugar

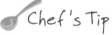 Chef's Tip

There is an enzyme in citrus fruit that will prevent gelatin from setting. Thus, when making jelly using citrus fruit, it is important to boil the fruit for at least 1 minute to destroy the enzyme. This applies to other fruit such as kiwi and pineapple as well.

1 Bloom gelatin in iced water for 1 minute, then remove and pat dry with a kitchen towel. Set aside. Slice grapefruit into halves.

2 Slice a small section off the base of grapefruit halves to enable grapefruit cups to stand. Spoon out grapefruit flesh.

3 Place grapefruit flesh in a strainer and squeeze to obtain 350 g juice. Place in a saucepan with lemon juice and boil over high heat for 1 minute.

4 Remove from heat and add sugar. Stir until dissolved. Add gelatin and repeat to stir until dissolved. Strain liquid in a bowl and place over a larger bowl of iced water.

5 Stir mixture until it thickens. Pour into grapefruit cups and refrigerate for at least 3 hours or until set. Garnish as desired before serving. Store refrigerated for up to 3 days.

CRÈME BRÛLÉE AU MASCARPONE

Makes 4 servings

This soft, creamy pudding is made using Italian mascarpone cheese.

Level of Difficulty: Easy

- **100 g egg yolks, at room temperature**
- **45 g sugar + more for crust**
- **80 g milk**
- **180 g heavy cream**
- **¼ pod vanilla bean, split lengthwise, seeds scraped**
- **160 g marscapone cheese, at room temperature**
- **20 g cream cheese, at room temperature**

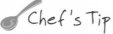 Chef's Tip

Timing is of utmost importance when preparing crème brûlée. Be sure to check and lightly shake the pudding after baking for 30 minutes. The centre should wobble. If not, continue baking for another 5 minutes and check again.

When preparing crème brûlée ahead of time, refrigerate it after step 7 and caramelise it only before serving. Without caramelising the top layer, crème brûlée will keep refrigerated for 2 days.

1 Preheat oven to 150°C. Place four 120-g ramekins in a deep baking tray. In a large bowl, whisk egg yolks and sugar until pale. Set aside.

2 In a small saucepan over medium heat, bring milk, heavy cream and vanilla seeds and pod to a simmer, stirring to mix. Remove from heat and set aside.

3 In a large bowl, whisk mascarpone and cream cheese together until smooth. Add warm milk mixture and whisk until smooth.

4 Add mascarpone, cream cheese and milk mixture to egg yolk mixture, half portion at a time, mixing well after each addition. Strain mixture into a bowl.

5 Spoon mixture evenly into prepared ramekins. Use a paper towel to remove any bubbles on surface of mixture to ensure crème brûlée is smooth.

6 Fill the baking tray with water to come halfway up the sides of ramekins. Bake for 35–40 minutes until mixture is set but still wobbly in the centre.

7 Remove ramekins from oven and place on a wire rack to cool for 15 minutes. When cool, refrigerate for at least 1 hour.

8 When ready to serve, sprinkle sugar on surface of crème brûlée and use a cook's blow torch to caramelise sugar. Serve immediately.

CHAMPAGNE JELLY

Makes 4 servings

This elegant dessert pairs a light champagne jelly with a lime-flavoured mousse.

Level of Difficulty: Easy

CHAMPAGNE JELLY

10 g gelatin sheet

450 ml champagne

85 g sugar

8 raspberries

LIME MOUSSE

2 g gelatin sheet

40 g water

10 g sugar

30 g heavy cream

1/2 lime, grated for zest and squeezed for juice

20 g egg white

8 g sugar

1 Prepare champagne jelly. Bloom gelatin in iced water for 1 minute, then remove and pat dry with a paper towel.

2 Heat 100 ml champagne in a heatproof bowl set over a pot of simmering water. Add gelatin and sugar and stir until dissolved.

3 Remove from heat and place over a bowl of iced water. Using a rubber spatula, stir until mixture thickens. Remove from iced water.

4 Fold remaining champagne into mixture. Divide half the mixture among 4 glasses. Drop 2 raspberries into each glass. Refrigerate for 10–15 minutes or until set.

5 Prepare lime mousse. Bloom gelatin as in step 1. Heat water with 10 g sugar to 100°C. Remove from heat. Stir in gelatin until dissolved. Strain and leave to cool.

6 Using a handheld mixer, whisk heavy cream at high speed until soft peaks form. Add cooled gelatin-syrup and lime zest and juice. Mix to combine. Set aside.

7 Using a handheld mixer, whisk egg white and 4 g sugar at high speed to soft peaks. Add remaining 4 g sugar and whisk until meringue is glossy and stiff.

8 Using a rubber spatula, scoop the meringue into the lime-cream mixture and fold to mix, scraping the base and sides of the bowl well.

9 Spoon lime mousse over set jelly. Chill for 30 minutes, then top with remaining jelly and chill for another 10–15 minutes until jelly is set. Garnish as desired. Serve or store refrigerated for up to 2 days.

AVOCADO MOUSSE

Makes 4 servings

This silky delicate mousse is topped with a tangy lemon jelly
that cuts the natural richness of the avocado.

Level of Difficulty: Easy

LEMON JELLY

5 g gelatin sheet

30 g sugar

175 g water

8 g honey

35 g lemon juice

AVOCADO MOUSSE

1¹/₂ ripe avocados

5 g gelatin sheet

190 g milk

40 g sugar

120 g heavy cream

10 g sugar

1 Prepare lemon jelly. Bloom
gelatin in iced water for 1 minute,
then remove and pat dry with a
paper towel. Set aside.

2 In a small saucepan over medium
heat, bring sugar, water and honey
to a boil. Remove from heat and
add gelatin, stirring until dissolved.

6 Bloom gelatin as in step 1.
Set aside. In a saucepan over
medium heat, heat milk and 40 g
sugar to 80°C. Remove from heat
and add gelatin, stirring until
dissolved.

7 Set saucepan over a bowl of
iced water and stir for about
3 minutes until mixture cools and
thickens. Remove from ice bath
and add to mashed avocado. Mix
well with a rubber spatula.

3 Strain mixture into a bowl and place into a larger bowl of iced water. Stir for about 3 minutes until mixture cools and thickens.

4 Remove from iced water and stir in lemon juice. Pour mixture into a shallow container. Cover and refrigerate for 2 hours or until set.

5 Prepare avocado mousse. Halve avocados. Using an ice cream scoop, remove seed and scoop out flesh into a bowl. Mash well. Set aside.

8 Using a hand whisk, whisk heavy cream and 10 g sugar until soft peaks form. Add avocado mixture and whisk until even. Spoon mousse into glasses, then refrigerate for 2 hours or until set.

9 To assemble, use a spoon to scrape and mince set jelly, then spoon a layer of jelly over set mousse. Garnish as desired and serve chilled. Store refrigerated for up to 1 day.

VANILLA BAVAROIS

Makes 8 servings

This delicate cream makes a light dessert served with fresh fruit or jam.

Level of Difficulty: Moderate

5 g gelatin sheet

100 g milk

$^1/_2$ **pod vanilla bean, split lengthwise, seeds scraped**

10 g sugar

30 g egg yolks, at room temperature

40 g sugar

350 g heavy cream

Chef's Tip

When heating the egg mixture (step 2), it is essential that it reaches 80°C for it to be safe to consume. Measure the temperature using a candy thermometer.

Work quickly and do not let the egg mixture stand for too long before whisking in the whipped cream as the gelatin will cause it to set.

1 Bloom gelatin in iced water for 1 minute. Remove and pat dry. Set aside. Simmer milk, vanilla seeds and pod and 10 g sugar in a saucepan over medium heat until mixture reaches 90°C. Set aside.

2 In a large bowl, whisk egg yolks and 40 g sugar until pale. Add warm milk and whisk until fully incorporated. Return mixture to saucepan and place over medium heat until mixture reaches 80°C.

3 Remove saucepan from heat. Using a hand whisk, whisk gelatin into mixture until dissolved. Strain mixture into another bowl and leave to cool until about 40°C.

4 Using a stand mixer, whisk heavy cream at high speed until soft peaks form. Switch to a hand whisk and whisk one-third of whipped cream into cooled egg yolk mixture.

5 Switch to a rubber spatula and continue to fold in remaining whipped cream until well mixed. Scrape base and sides of bowl thoroughly.

6 Ladle cream into serving cups or wine glasses and refrigerate for at least 2 hours to set. Garnish as desired or with fresh fruit or jam before serving.

Chocolate

TEMPERING CHOCOLATE

POINTS TO NOTE

* Use at least 500 g chocolate to make the process of tempering easier.

* If using a block of chocolate, chop it finely using a serrated knife so the chocolate melts more readily. Alternatively, use chocolate buttons.

* A candy thermometer is an essential tool as you will need to measure the temperature of the chocolate at various points.

* Use a clean and dry heatproof bowl when tempering chocolate as the chocolate will turn lumpy if it comes into contact with water.

A STEP-BY-STEP GUIDE

1   Heat water in a medium saucepan until it reaches 60°C–80°C. Set a heatproof bowl over the saucepan of simmering water.

2   Add the chocolate and mix slowly using a rubber spatula until the chocolate is smooth and melted and reaches 50°C.

3   In a bowl of similar size, add ice and water until one-third full.

4   Place bowl with melted chocolate over the ice bath and fold chocolate with a rubber spatula until it cools to 28°C and thickens.

5   Reheat the medium saucepan of water until simmering.

6   Set the bowl of chocolate over the saucepan of simmering water and fold the chocolate until it reaches 31°C–32°C.

7   The chocolate is now ready for coating or moulding.

CHOCOLATE ALMONDS

Makes 70–80 pieces

Chocolate almonds are easily purchased but nothing beats making your own!

Level of Difficulty: Difficult

50 g sugar

15 g water

100 g roasted almonds with skin

10 g salted butter

Canola oil for brushing

100 g dark chocolate buttons (58% cocoa)

Cocoa powder for coating

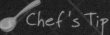

Chef's Tip

To roast raw almonds, preheat the oven to 160°C. Spread the almonds out on a tray and roast for 10–12 minutes.

When coating the almonds with chocolate, it is important to do it gradually, adding just a small portion of chocolate at a time. This is to ensure that the chocolate adheres to the almonds evenly. If too much chocolate is added at once, it will tend to stick to the bowl instead of the almonds.

1 In a small saucepan, heat sugar and water to 115°C. Remove from heat and add almonds. Mix with a wooden spoon until evenly coated and mixture is cool and white.

2 Return saucepan to medium heat and stir lightly until sugar caramelises and turns brown. Remove from heat. Add butter and stir until well mixed.

3 Carefully spread almonds out on a baking tray brushed lightly with canola oil. Leave to cool to room temperature. In the meantime, temper chocolate (page 109).

4 Transfer cooled almonds to a bowl. Add tempered chocolate a quarter portion at a time and mix well after each addition until almonds are well coated.

5 Add cocoa powder to coat almonds, then pour almonds into a sieve to remove any excess cocoa powder. Store in an airtight container for up to 2 weeks.

NAMA CHOCOLATE

Makes 36 pieces

This Japanese treat is popular because of its smooth, silky texture and it is not difficult to do at home. Try it.

Level of Difficulty: Easy

180 g milk chocolate buttons (30–40% cocoa)

180 g dark chocolate buttons (58% cocoa)

238 g heavy cream

13 g glucose

67 g cocoa butter

Cocoa powder for dusting

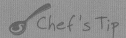

Chef's Tip

To ensure that the resulting chocolate is smooth and silky, it is essential that the cocoa butter is melted separately, then whisked into the chocolate and cream mixture (step 3).

1 Place milk chocolate and dark chocolate buttons into a large bowl. Set aside. In small saucepan over medium heat, bring heavy cream and glucose to a simmer, stirring slowly.

2 Remove heavy cream from heat and pour over chocolate buttons. Stir with a whisk, starting from inside out, until chocolate melts and mixture is smooth and even. Set aside.

3 In another small saucepan over low heat, add cocoa butter and let it melt. Remove from heat and leave to cool until 50°C. Whisk into chocolate mixture until well mixed.

4 Using a rubber spatula, scrape base and sides of bowl thoroughly until fully incorporated and mixture is even. Line a shallow 18-cm square baking tray with plastic wrap.

5 Pour mixture into tray. Refrigerate overnight to set. When set, cut chocolate into 3-cm squares and dust with cocoa powder. Store refrigerated for up to 2 weeks.

CHOCOLATE GÂTEAU

Makes one 15-cm round cake

This rich chocolate cake will satisfy any chocolate lover.

Level of Difficulty: Moderate

100 g dark chocolate buttons (58% cocoa)

100 g unsalted butter, at room temperature

3 eggs, yolks and whites separated

100 g sugar

55 g pastry flour, sifted

Icing sugar for dusting

Chef's Tip

When adding the pastry flour, be sure to mix well to activate the gluten, which is necessary to achieve the rich and dense texture of gâteau cakes.

1 Preheat oven to 200°C. Line a 15-cm round baking tin with parchment paper, leaving a 2-cm overhang. Fill a pot with water up to 4 cm high and simmer over medium heat.

2 Melt chocolate and butter in a heatproof bowl placed over simmering water. Stir until well mixed. Remove from heat. Add egg yolks one at a time, whisking constantly. Set aside.

3 Prepare meringue. Using a handheld mixer, whisk together egg whites and sugar at high speed until soft peaks form.

4 Using a rubber spatula, fold one-third of meringue into chocolate mixture until fully incorporated. Fold in pastry flour and mix well.

5 Fold in remaining meringue in two additions, ensuring full incorporation after each addition. Transfer batter to prepared tin.

6 Bake for 10 minutes, then lower oven temperature to 160°C and bake for 20–25 minutes, until a skewer inserted into centre of cake comes out clean.

7 Remove from oven and leave to cool for 15 minutes. When cool enough to handle, unmould cake and peel off parchment paper.

8 Leave cake to cool completely. Dust cake with icing sugar and decorate as desired before serving. Store refrigerated for up to 2 days.

Celebration Cakes

GREEN TEA AND AZUKI ROLL CAKE

Makes one 30-cm long roll cake

The lightly bitter taste of green tea is perfectly matched with the sweetness of the red bean paste, creating a winning combination in this roll cake.

Level of Difficulty: Moderate

Chantilly cream (page 122)

Canned sweet chestnuts and fresh blueberries for decoration

Green tea powder for dusting

GREEN TEA ROLL SPONGE

55 g pastry flour

5 g green tea powder

180 g eggs

90 g sugar

20 g unsalted butter

40 g milk

RED BEAN CREAM

180 g heavy cream

20 g sugar

50 g red bean paste

1 Preheat oven to 180°C. Line a shallow 30-cm square baking tray with parchment paper, leaving a 2-cm overhang. Sift together pastry flour and green tea powder onto a sheet of parchment paper.

2 Fill a pot with water up to 4 cm high and simmer over medium heat. In a heatproof bowl, whisk eggs and sugar lightly. Place over simmering water and whisk constantly in large strokes until mixture reaches 40°C.

6 Pour batter into prepared baking tray. Using a flat scraper, gently smoothen surface of batter in one direction. Bake for 10–12 minutes or until surface of sponge is brown.

7 Test if sponge is done by pressing the centre lightly. It should spring back. Place sponge on a wire rack. Peel away parchment paper at the side. Leave to cool for about 30 minutes.

8 Prepare red bean cream. Using a stand mixer, whisk heavy cream and sugar at high speed until soft peaks form. Add red bean paste and whisk at medium speed for 5 seconds.

3 Transfer mixture to the bowl of a stand mixer and whisk at high speed until mixture doubles in volume and turns very pale. Set aside. Heat butter and milk in a microwave oven on High for 30 seconds. Stir to mix.

4 Turn mixer speed to low and add half the warm butter and milk mixture. Beat for 5 seconds, then increase to high speed and beat until mixture is doubled in volume.

5 Using a rubber spatula, fold in sifted flour and green tea powder until fully incorporated. Fold in remaining warm butter and milk mixture. Scrape base and sides of bowl thoroughly. Do not over mix.

9 To peel off parchment paper at bottom of sponge, place a cutting board over the sponge and flip it over. Peel off parchment paper and flip sponge back upright. Place on a large sheet of parchment paper. Spread sponge with red bean cream.

10 Using a long knife, make a line parallel to one side of the cake, 2 cm from the edge. Use this line as the starting point to roll up the cake. Roll cake up together with parchment paper, using a long ruler to keep the roll straight.

11 Keep cake wrapped up and refrigerate for at least 30 minutes. Trim ends of cake, then decorate with Chantilly cream, sweet chestnuts and blueberries. Dust with green tea powder. Store refrigerated for up to 2 days.

FRUIT ROLL

Makes one 30-cm long roll cake

An all-time favourite, this fruit roll is filled
with Chantilly cream and mixed tropical fruit.

Level of Difficulty: Easy

1 roll sponge (page 36),
chilled

1 cup mixed diced fruit,
such as kiwi, pineapple,
strawberry, mango
and/or peach

Fresh fruit for decoration

Icing sugar for dusting

CHANTILLY CREAM

200 g heavy cream

15 g sugar

1 Prepare Chantilly cream. In a
mixing bowl and using a handheld
mixer, whisk heavy cream and
sugar at high speed until soft
peaks form.

2 Place sponge on a large sheet
of parchment paper. Spoon
three-quarters of Chantilly cream
onto sponge and spread evenly
using an offset spatula.

3 Top with a layer of diced fruit.
Using a long knife, make a line
parallel to one side of the cake,
2 cm from the edge. Use this line
as the starting point to roll up
the cake.

4 Roll cake up together with
parchment paper, using a long
ruler to keep the roll straight.
Keep cake wrapped up and
refrigerate for at least 30 minutes.

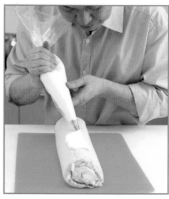

5 Transfer remaining Chantilly
cream to a piping bag fitted with
0.8-cm round tip. Trim ends of
cake, then decorate with cream
and fresh fruit. Dust with icing
sugar. Consume within the day.

STRAWBERRY SHORTCAKE

Makes one 18-cm round cake

This Japanese style strawberry shortcake is made up of soft sponge, Chantilly cream and fresh strawberries. It is the most popular choice for birthday cakes in Japan.

Level of Difficulty: Difficult

1 round sponge, 18-cm, (page 38)

Strawberries, as needed, washed and hulled, some halved, some left whole

Icing sugar for dusting

CHANTILLY CREAM

400 g heavy cream

20 g sugar

Chef's Tip

Do not leave whipped cream at room temperature for too long or it will melt. When not using immediately, keep it refrigerated.

1 Cut sponge horizontally into half. Prepare Chantilly cream. In a mixing bowl and using a handheld mixer, whisk heavy cream and sugar at high speed until soft peaks form.

2 Spoon a quarter of Chantilly cream into another bowl and continue to whisk until medium soft. Spoon half the medium soft cream onto bottom half of sponge and spread evenly.

3 Arrange strawberry halves evenly over layer of cream, then spread over remaining medium soft cream. Place top half of sponge over cream and strawberry layer.

4 Using a hand whisk, whisk half the remaining soft cream until medium soft. Spoon on top of cake and use a metal spatula to spread cream over top and sides of cake.

5 Whisk remaining soft cream until medium soft. Transfer to a piping bag fitted with a 1-cm round tip. Decorate cake with cream and strawberries. Dust with icing sugar. Refrigerate for 30 minutes before serving. Consume within the day.

SOUFFLÉ CHEESECAKE

Makes one 18-cm round cake

Unlike traditional cheesecakes, soufflé cheesecakes are light and airy.

Level of Difficulty: Moderate

1 round sponge, 18 x 0.5-cm (page 38)

300 g cream cheese, at room temperature

3 eggs, yolks and whites separated

24 g pastry flour, sifted

75 g milk

75 g heavy cream

1/2 lemon, grated for zest and squeezed for 30 g juice

60 g sugar

Icing sugar for dusting

Chef's Tip

When incorporating the meringue into the batter, fold briskly and be careful not to deflate the meringue or the cake will lose its light and airy texture.

1 Preheat oven to 200°C. Line an 18-cm round baking tin with parchment paper, leaving a 2-cm overhang. Place sponge into base of baking tin. Set aside.

2 In a large bowl and using a hand whisk, whisk cream cheese until smooth. Add 2 egg yolks and whisk until incorporated, then whisk in remaining egg yolk.

6 Bake for 15–20 minutes until the top of cake is light brown. Lower oven temperature to 160°C and continue baking for another 40–45 minutes.

7 Test if cake is done by pressing the centre of cake lightly. It should spring back. Remove baking tin from water bath and leave to cool for 5 minutes.

3 Whisk in flour. Set aside. Bring milk and heavy cream to a simmer over low heat. Add to batter and whisk until fully incorporated. Mix in lemon zest and juice. Set aside.

4 Prepare meringue. In a large bowl and using a handheld mixer, whisk egg whites and sugar at high speed until white and still runny.

5 Fold meringue into batter half portion at a time. Pour into prepared tin and place in a deep baking tray. Fill tray with water to come 1 cm up the side of tin.

8 Turn cake onto a plate and peel off parchment paper. Leave to cool, then cover with a plastic container and refrigerate for 2 hours before serving.

9 Dust cake with icing sugar and decorate if desired just before serving. This soufflé can be kept refrigerated for up to 2 days.

FRUIT CHARLOTTE

Makes one 18-cm round cake

This beautiful cake is made with creamy bavarois and crisp biscuits à la cuillère topped with fresh fruit.

Level of Difficulty: Moderate

1 portion biscuits à la cuillère dough (page 40), chilled

Icing sugar for dusting

2 round sponges, each 18 x 1-cm, (page 38)

1 portion Chantilly cream (page 80)

Cut fruit of choice

VANILLA BAVAROIS

6 g gelatin sheet

120 g milk

1/3 pod vanilla bean, split lengthwise, seeds scraped

10 g sugar

30 g egg yolks

15 g sugar

100 g heavy cream

Chef's Tip

Unlike the recipe for the vanilla bavarois dessert (page 104), this bavarois requires only a small amount of whipped cream and so it can be folded in all at once.

1 Preheat oven to 200°C. Line a baking tray. Transfer dough to a piping bag fitted with a 1.5-cm round tip. Pipe 6-cm lines, keeping them close to each other, on prepared baking tray.

2 Dust dough well with icing sugar and let rest for 1–2 minutes, then dust again lightly. Bake for 10–12 minutes until biscuits start to crack and are hard on the outside. Transfer to a wire rack.

6 Return mixture to saucepan and place over medium heat until mixture reaches 80°C. Remove from heat. Add gelatin and whisk until gelatin is dissolved.

7 Strain mixture into a large bowl and leave to cool until about 40°C. As mixture is cooling, whisk heavy cream at high speed until soft peaks form.

3 Line an 18-cm round cake tin with parchment paper. Place cooled biscuits into prepared cake tin to line the side. Fit a sponge round into the base of cake tin. Set aside.

4 Prepare vanilla bavarois. Bloom gelatin in iced water for 1 minute. Remove and pat dry. In a small saucepan over medium heat, heat milk, vanilla seeds and pod and 10 g sugar to 90°C.

5 In a medium bowl, whisk together egg yolks and 15 g sugar until pale. Gradually add warm milk mixture while whisking and continue to whisk until fully incorporated.

8 When mixture is cool, whisk in whipped cream, then pour into cake tin. Top with other sponge round and press down evenly. Refrigerate for at least 2 hours.

9 To release cake from tin, turn tin over and use your hand to support cake. Decorate with Chantilly cream and fruit of choice. Serve chilled. Store refrigerated for up to 1 day.

Choux

PARISIENNE

Makes 12–15 puffs

Filled with a soft and smooth vanilla custard cream, these golden choux puffs make a perfect teatime snack.

Level of Difficulty: Moderate

1 portion (250 g) pâte à choux
  dough (page 30)

1 egg, lightly beaten

300 g diced almonds

Sugar for topping

Icing sugar for dusting

CHANTILLY CREAM

100 g heavy cream

1 portion custard cream
  (page 28)

Chef's Tip

When lowering the oven temperature, do not open the oven door or the puffs will deflate.

1 Preheat oven to 200°C. Transfer choux dough to a piping bag fitted with a 0.8-cm round tip. Pipe 4-cm wide, 2-cm high rounds on a lined baking tray, spacing them 3 cm apart.

2 Using a pastry brush, bush choux rounds lightly with beaten egg. Using a wet fork, lightly shape rounds to smoothen the surface. Top with diced almonds and sugar.

3 Bake for 15–18 minutes until dough has risen slightly. Lower oven temperature to 180°C and continue baking for 28–30 minutes, until choux puffs are golden brown.

4 Remove from oven and place puffs on a wire rack to cool. Once puffs are cool, use a small sharp knife to cut each puff in half. Do not cut through. Set aside.

5 Prepare Chantilly cream. Whisk heavy cream at high speed for 3 minutes until soft peaks form. Fold whipped cream into custard cream until smooth.

6 Transfer Chantilly cream to a piping bag fitted with a 1-cm round tip and fill puffs with cream. Dust with icing sugar before serving. Consume within the day.

PARIS-BREST

Makes one 16-cm round pastry

This French dessert was created in 1891 to commemorate the Paris-Brest bicycle race, hence its resemblance to a bicycle wheel.

Level of Difficulty: Moderate

Flour for marking

1 portion (250 g) pâte à choux dough (page 30)

1 egg, lightly beaten

100 g sliced almonds

5 small bananas, peeled

Icing sugar for dusting

PRALINE CREAM

100 g praline paste

100 g unsalted butter, at room temperature

300 g custard cream (page 28)

Chef's Tip

When piping the choux dough rounds, be sure to start at different points for each circle so that the surface of the pastry will be even when baked.

When lowering the oven temperature, do not open the oven door or the puffs will deflate.

1 Preheat oven to 200°C. Line 2 baking trays with parchment paper. Mark a 16-cm diameter circle on each sheet of parchment paper (using the lid of a pot dipped in flour).

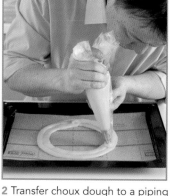

2 Transfer choux dough to a piping bag fitted with a 1-cm round tip. Pipe a line within the circle, another on the outer circumference and a third on top of where the two rounds meet.

3 Using a pastry brush, brush rounds lightly with beaten egg. Using a wet fork, lightly shape rounds to smoothen the surface, then coat with sliced almonds.

4 Bake for 15–18 minutes until dough has risen slightly. Lower oven temperature to 180°C and bake for 28–30 minutes, until choux puff is golden brown. Leave to cool.

5 Prepare praline cream. In a large bowl, mix praline paste with a hand whisk until smooth. Add butter and mix until combined. Mix in custard cream until just incorporated.

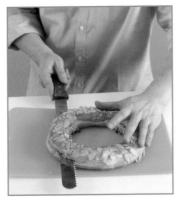

6 Transfer praline cream to a piping bag fitted with a 1-cm round tip. Cut cooled pastry horizontally. Set top layer aside. Pipe praline cream onto bottom layer of pastry.

7 Top with bananas, then pipe more cream over bananas. Sandwich with top layer of pastry. Lightly dust with icing sugar before serving. Consume within the day.

CHOCOLATE ÉCLAIRS

Makes 16–18 éclairs, each about 12 cm long

These finger-shaped pastries are filled with chocolate and
Chantilly cream and topped with a layer of chocolate ganache.

Level of Difficulty: Easy

**1 portion (250 g) pâte à choux
dough (page 30)**

1 egg, lightly beaten

CHOCOLATE CREAM

30 g dark chocolate buttons

100 g custard cream (page 28)

GANACHE

70 g dark chocolate buttons

70 g heavy cream

CHANTILLY CREAM

100 g heavy cream

Chef's Tip

Melting chocolate in the
microwave oven is fast and
convenient, but extra care must
be taken so the chocolate does
not burn, especially when working
with small quantities of chocolate.

1 Preheat oven to 200°C. Line a
baking tray. Transfer choux dough
to a piping bag fitted with a 1-cm
round tip. Pipe dough into logs
about 10 cm long and 1 cm high,
spacing them 4 cm apart.

2 Using a pastry brush, lightly
brush dough with beaten egg.
Using a wet fork, lightly shape
dough to smoothen surface. Bake
for 15–18 minutes or until dough
has risen slightly.

6 Prepare ganache. Place dark
chocolate in a bowl. In a saucepan,
bring heavy cream to a simmer until
it reaches 90°C. Pour over dark
chocolate and whisk to combine.

7 Slice cooled choux pastry logs
into half horizontally. Dip top layer
of logs in ganache and arrange on
a baking tray. Refrigerate for
10 minutes until ganache is set.

3 Lower oven temperature to 180°C and continue baking for 28–30 minutes until choux puffs are risen and golden brown. Remove from oven and leave to cool on a wire rack.

4 Prepare chocolate cream. Place chocolate buttons in a microwave-safe bowl and heat in a microwave oven on High at 20-second bursts, stirring and checking each time, so chocolate does not burn.

5 When chocolate is smooth and melted, fold it into custard cream and mix well. Transfer chocolate cream to a piping bag fitted with a 0.8-cm round tip. Set aside.

8 Meanwhile, prepare Chantilly cream. Using a hand whisk, whisk heavy cream until soft peaks form. Transfer to a piping bag fitted with a 0.8-cm round tip.

9 Pipe a thick layer of chocolate cream onto choux bases, then pipe a layer of Chantilly cream over. Sandwich with top layer and serve. Consume within the day.

たのしんで！